STAR THISTLE
& Other Poems

By Lisa Summers

FMRL
Berkeley, California

Star Thistle & Other Poems

© 2012 by Lisa Summers
All rights reserved.

ISBN-13: 978-0-9671001-4-2
Library of Congress Control Number: 2013930914

FMRL
P.O. Box 5124 Berkeley CA 94705
fmrl.com. | info@fmrl.com | 510 992 3675

Daedalus Howell, Publisher
Kit Fergus, Designer

Printed in the United States of America

Grateful acknowledgement is made to the following publications in which a few (a very few) of these poems appeared: *zaum*, *Kubla Khan*, *Atlanta Review*, *Dark River Press*.

NOTES: "Once I was Queen of the Rubbish Heap" is a "found poem" based on Christina Rossetti's "Dream Land." Likewise, "Weather Vane" is a rearrangement of select lines from the Wikipedia entry for "weather-vanes" and "Wide Sufficing Sea" is scavenged from William Carlos Williams's "Asphodel, That Greeny Flower."

Follow Lisa Summers on Twitter @the_bananafish.

STAR THISTLE
& Other Poems

By Lisa Summers

FMRL
Berkeley, California

I

Harpies   2
Flight Through Ashdown Forest   4
Our Lady of Palabras Perdidas   6
The Confession Of Ariadne   10
Underwear For The Afterlife   14
Pysche   16

II

Carcass Island   20
La Sirena   21
Beyond The Farallones   22
The End Of Consonance   23
Tsunami   24
Miranda   26
The Moon Was A Ghastly Galleon   27
Tides   28
Hollow Men, Shallow Men   30

III

My Uncles Are Men Of Stones   32
Radiant City   34
The Living Bridges Of Megahlaya   36
The Orphan   37

IV

Blue Skinned Man   40
In Another Life   42
Jump Rope Rhyme Of The Moirae   43
Once I Was Queen of a Rubbish Heap   44
The Wide Sufficing Sea   45
Weather Vane   46

V

Monstrous Teachers   48
Still Life With Object(s)   51
The Quotidian Inferno   53
The Young Master and the Lotus   55
Star Thistle   57
Six Haiku   59
De Poésie Ou De Vertu   61
Kehoe   63
Jerusalem Cricket   65
The Locusts   66
House Finches   67

VI

I - The Dutch Finger Prince   70
II – The Stonemason's Wife   72
III – The Widow's Harvest   74

VII

The Nightjar (Alba)   78
Our Last Speakeasy Days   79
A Brief History Of Mirrors   80
A Brief History Of Echoes   82

VIII

Laconia   86

For my daughters and sons
with special thanks to Dr. T

"from what we cannot hold the stars are made"
– W.S. Merwin, *Youth*

I

Harpies

The Mind Abhors What the Eyes Adore.
Consider the case of the Sisters Domingo,
Unholy Wingéd Birds of the Double Wide:
a front yard flock of pink flamingos, wading
among the cigarette butts, dry dead grass.

Imagine a string of Christmas lights
strung between the telephone pole and
a half-chopped pine spiked with nails,
the smell of creosote and Salem slims.

You'd know the place by the scent of grease,
by the torn stars and stripes rotting
under black hollows of the juniper bushes–

the primer grey El Camino on cinder blocks,
the tennis balls stuffed down old tube socks
for a blind bull terrier named 'Cookie Jim'
in memory of the Sisters' meth-headed brother
who flew the coop when the rent came due.

Whenever a skittish postman, or
the mute meter reader from the gas company
on scheduled rounds happens by,
the Sisters Domingo shriek and shout
flap around the yard, foam about the mouth.

They steal meat from the Liquor Shack
where a man rumored to be an exiled king
works the counter, secretly feeding
the mongrels and rats from his paltry stores.

With their coral, chipped-paint talons
they can fire an empty Schlitz or a can
of spray-on cheese fast as a split-finger fastball.

On the day Jason finally sees fit to set a match
to the shake roof, a final hush descends; light as
snowflakes, the ashes of the burning trailer fall.
Mongrels, rats and Cookie Jim gather,
drawn to the acrid stench of stolen meat.

Passersby Beware!
Clawed feet and swollen, feathered bellies,
[the Sisters Domingo] *caw their lamentations
in the eerie trees.*

Flight Through Ashdown Forest

Jump across the river stones
Catch the silver fish –
From your pocket throw the stolen bones
To make your final wish!

Summon all young maidens
To the sides of noble men
At Bloody Bolebroke Castle –
The King said once again

Hide inside the thickets
Tho thorns tear at your feet –
By the gate of golden crickets
Is where the two roads meet

Come hither all young maidens
To the house of noble men
At Bloody Bolebroke Castle –
The King said once again

Go by smoky cûs fordh where
The fox hides from the hound –
Down the cold hidden lane
By the wintry dour downs

Stitch up all young maidens
To the skin of noble men
At Bloody Bolebroke Castle –
The King said once again

With your cloaks a'torn and muddied
Past the burning Tan Caer Lake,
Find the mossy, cut-stone cottage
Where the kindly crone now waits

Flay the flying maidens
With the swords of noble men
At Bloody Bolebroke Castle!
The King said once again

By the broken garden gate
Find the path laid by Naw Meyn
That, under sleeping apple-wood,
Winds to mist-veiled Avalon

Taken are our maidens
By the fairies, noble men;
Bolebroke's but a boudshi!
The King said once again

Notes:
From *Celtic Cornish Places Names*
http://cornish-place-names.wikidot.com/jago-celtic

Boudshi. A cow-house.
Naw meyn. The nine stones: from naw, nine, meyn, stones.
Tan caer Lake. The fire castle lake: from tan, fire, caer, a castle
Cûs fordh. The way by the wood: from cûs, wood, fordh, a way.

Bolebroke Castle is the name of Henry VIII's hunting lodge where he courted his second wife Ann Boleyn

Our Lady of Palabras Perdidas

Parte I

Olden, yea! But a bobbish yet, I is.
"Vagabunda!" They shouts, hands over ears.

"Conservadora!" I say to kindred scavengers,
Who have taken to calling me, in such times –
  Our Lady of Palabras Perdidas

Their language be but sad, cag-mag
Rummagin' in Latin shards n' splinters.
"Nuestra Senora, where came you from?"
They me ask

"Ahhhh," and here I point North and East
With a stick of smooth olive wood;
"When the hills were still young and stupid,
I was married over the broomstick to a quaddy lad;
Many, many years back, he died.
Yea, I've since grown a good-sized back hump –
A hillock cloaked in gray!" I say.

"I've no whingle, and I'm no drumble!" Meh.
I make me way scavenging in the rubbish heaps
for las palabras perdidas – unwanted and fluey
made Time's poor orphan,
him's but a proud Costermonger

But when ye rub 'em up, make 'em shine
Even such a one as meself, of deep wrine can see
Under the oily tarnish and the stain

Ye know what they says (a flourish of me hands)
"*Verba Volant, scripta manent* – words fly, but writings remain!
Yadda, yadda, yadda."

Parte II

In one heap Me found a birdish Burdalane
The last one, poor wee lass, surviving of her kin
Cark, she were, and thought a cumberground

"But now, now dear!" I said. "Our Lady
will make ye a shake-down of fine feathers
and new spring grass, with whittles o'white petals
and draughts from yon clear, running brook
before yer queachy young bones sleepaway."

Her laughter flowed like music – a sweet rindle
A small pebble kept she in her mouth
lest felth become strength, its ugesome successor.

It were by chance me found her here, Mnemosyne
– Beloved Eldmother –
And muse of old and wordly women;
I pulled her up from her Earth-fast taproots
but she, forswunk and grown lanken
began to speak but clyted.

Her voice was wantsome from moss and rust –
she'd become elden, and dwined
under a wasted of letters and her long sloom:

"These young and fluttersome moffles –
What do they know of a word's wroth?"

We drank tea and eftsoons she spake again:
"Ne'er a word ran deeper than sewers of ruined cities
Nor does history disturb a taproot or a deep-sea clam.
All language will ever be in the heaps."

DEFINITIONS
Bobbish…to be in good health
Burdalane…the last child surviving in a family
Cag-Mag…decaying meat
Cark…to be fretfully anxious
Clyte…An orator who – for want of a word or an idea suddenly stops in his speech and sits down, has clyted.
Costermonger…a greengrocer or seller of produce
Crine…to shrink, or become smaller from drying up (the diminutive is "crinkle")
Cumberground…something that's totally worthless and in the way
Darg…a day's work
Drumble…Someone who does a thing in a way that makes it clear that he or she has no idea how to do it is drumbling.
Dwine…to pine away or waste away, slowly (the diminutive is "dwindle")
Earth-fast…"firm in the earth and difficult to be moved"
Elden…to grow old
Eldmother…grandmother, ancestor

Felth…the power of feeling in the fingers
Fleuy…dusty
Forswunk…completely worn out with work
Lanken…to grow thin and lean
Moffle…to do something badly and with no idea how it ought to be done
Over the Broomstick….to be married in a folk ceremony, unrecognized by the law
Quaddy…short and thick
Queachy…shaking, quivering
Rindle…to sparkle like running water
Shakedown…bed
Sleepaway…to die peacefully and gradually without being sick and without suffering
Sloom…to sleep soundly and heavily (distinguished from "slumber," which Mackay says is to sleep lightly)
Whingle…to complain
Whittles…vittles, or food
Wrine…a deep line in the face (the diminutive is "wrinkle")

And all the old "-some" adjectives, like…
Bendsome…pliable, yielding
Fluttersome…quick, agile, restless
Foulsome…foul, disgusting
Hindersome…holding things back, in the way, delaying
Janglesome…quarrelsome
Longsom…tedious
Lugsome…difficult to move along, heavy
Sweltersome…hot and sultry and close, of weather
Tanglesome…unreasonable in arguments
Ugsome…ugly
Wantsome…deficient, lacking

The Confession Of Ariadne

A small brass bell
hung from a plain red string,
from the knob of the glass door
at a dimly lit café

it jingled brightly when she came in,
softly singing, singing to herself, and
smelling of sweet seapink and jasmine

Ariadne, Mistress of the Labyrinth
took a seat at my table by the wall;
she took off her shawl
woven from reeds and a ball of twine

"We thought that you were –
I said. "Hanging from a tree."

"Poor, poor Ariadne," answered she
a hand on her fair head,
cruelly mocking my sympathy.

"Such speculations! Such false accusations!
in case you have notions preconceived
about my past, my heart, my selfless deeds,
let me tell you something about Labyrinths:

If I may, before we begin, you know
it's not the getting out that counts,
what counts is getting in!

the seven boys and girls by kingly orders
were taken from Athenian borders, then

sent to the morbid shores of Crete –
Minos' offering to the Minotaur of meat,
who, history forgets, was my beloved brother
Queen Pasiphae, our beloved mother;

You know the story–

she, with her ill-famed choice of mates,
bid Daedalus build a wooden crate
to fulfill those bestial passions
(the lust of Poseidon)

still, behind the cloak of history hides
the man inside a bull's disguise
wanton, yes! yet my mother was no fool –
think! why else might a man be called a bull?

so she conceived a sweet young boy – Asterion,
who she loved like any mother loves her son
and who Minos, in his shame
gave the boy a foul and hateful name:
Minotaur –

pausing to consider, Ariadne confessed
before continuing with the rest

– they say I gave Theseus two things –
a sword and a certain length of string
so that he might retrace heroic steps
through the dark and perilous depths
of the great Knossian Labyrinth
from whose dark twists and fateful turns
no living man had yet returned.

"Here," said Ariadne, "the key word is man;
A sister is a different matter; a sister can
pay a visit to her beastly brother
to bear some kisses from his worried mother
who thinks only of her lonely son
and in silence weeps
but in the deepest black
of one night creeps –

Ariadne swept aside her long black hair
and spoke
with conspiratorial flair

"In the company of nine great men
and her clever daughter
we carved a tunnel to the turquoise water
through the deep stone walls
of those dank and seeping halls

as for Minos – Daedalus did not love the man
who ruled with cruel and heavy hands,
and so he left a piece undone
of his great maze, yet not a one
but he who dwelt there knew

and thus, when poor Athenian youths
were banished to their savage deaths
they did not take a final breath
at the hands nor the horns of the Minotaur
but followed the dim light of stars
to Naxos

by boat we went at night
there, we built an earthly Paradise;
side by side we worked under sun and sky
until one strong man, he caught my eye,
despite his mighty stature, let us say
he was as docile as a cow, (in many of his ways);
but a man, he proved himself to be
not a glory-seeking founder-king
like Theseus, who left me a "lover spurned"
yet still adorns the pot and urn.

it's said of poor Ariadne, that Dionysus
by his wineherd's art
with lusty in his punchdrunk heart,
claimed a princess for his own.
Oh, Lucky Me!"
Ariadne groaned.

"No, I could not stand his sour breath
the spilt wine stench on hairy breast,
nor did I hang myself in deep despair;
Theseus, with his hero's badge – what did he care?
His love was cold and slightly stony;
as for me, I prefer
a stalwart bull
to any one-trick pony!

Underwear For The Afterlife

When I was in the Underworld
I remembered something weird
My Mother used to tell me –

"Before getting into a car, dear,
Always make sure, have a care
Your underwear is clean and decent;
You never know when you might be in an accident,
Pinned to a tree with the wheels still spinning,
Still turning with the car sideways in the ditch
Or flipped over a cliff.
You never know when an
Eligible bachelor, maybe one of those
Brave Blue-Suited Firemen or Paramedics
Might have to use the Jaws of Life
To cut you from the wreckage.

And even if your friend is dead
And spread along the highway in bits,
Limbs in the thickets and drainage ditches,
Her limp body slung over the center divider-
You never know when
They might still have to cut your clothes off YOU;

You know how hard it is,
When the blood and gravel mix in
With glass shards in your skin,
To get the clothes off to check
For further injuries.

So, my dear, have a care what you wear –

No teddies made of gummy bears
No rubber-studded negligees,
No Superhero lingerie or
Or chocolate covered bustiers
No furry thongs, no leather belts
No corsets made of weasel pelts
No babydolls, no black silk slips
No paste-on cups in the shape of lips
No super-conducting underwire
No French Maid or High School Nurse attire
No garter belts or Union suits
No bloomers made from parachutes

Because, wouldn't it be a shame
For some handsome ambulance driver
With a steady job, a promising future,
To catch you so very ill-prepared,
Wearing the wrong sort of underwear?"

When I was in the Underworld,
Even with my chattering teeth
And my blood as cold as ice,
I remembered then her strange advice:
"You know it's never what's outside that counts
But the person underneath!
If you want to catch a decent man,
Dear, stick to cotton briefs."

Pysche

Listen, fair maidens, the soul is but a tenant
In the bones and coursing blood;
The flesh does not house the soul,
And the soul is not made whole
By any messengers of Love.

My case is no different –
(Tho my rooms be well-appointed.)

My Eros, my fabled fate –
Quiver and bow on his back
Wingéd poster boy of amorous pain!
So pale and flaccid
Overfed on his mother's vain milk
To think, as she did, t'would be my end
To marry an ugly man
A coarse brute with rough hands,
Fit for spade and plough,
But with a serene mind and tho,
His heart would n'er be full of love,
He would not scorn the pace
Of passing seasons on my face;
But would find me ever more Psyche
In my own garden where I dwelt in peace

That Love and Soul make one
Let me disabuse you! My soul is my own.
Let me tell you a story –

Fearing my betrothal to a monster
Wishing to secure a proper match,

My mother sought the oracle,
Who said it was foreseen by the Fates
That I would meet this beast
Upon the craggy mountain top
And that would be the end of poor Psyche

Not so, maidens. Not so.

It came to pass that Zephyr, my sister
Bore me away on her kindly wind
To a meadow of soft grass, where a great forest rose
At the Western border; there
Eros called me to a fine castle
Where the rooms within were all empty
And all mine.
Not one contained a single mirror.
Yet the sunlight on the floor,
Gentle kisses of the West wind,
And the rustling in the trees
All sufficed for me.

(Besides, if given the choice,
Eros always did prefer boys.)

And as for his plotting mother –
Vain Aphrodite!
Jealous Dutchess of bones and blood and pus

Well, Eros and I
We kept our little secret
Between the two of us.

II

Carcass Island

Come away to Carcass Island
In the sundering, southern seas
Where black Night Heron shadows
Roost in scorched-wood cypress trees

Come away to Carcass Island
Where the tussock grasses die
Among the dog roses and fuschias
Under high, cerulean skies

Come away to Carcass Island
Where the ghosts hum funeral hymns
And the sailors sway like ragdolls
From noose-knots hung from limbs

Come away to Carcass Island
Where cabbage palms once grew
For I've never known an Anyone
More dearly dead than you

La Sirena

I sailed upon the Seven Seas
Long afore ye were ever born
'Til we were caught upon th'aigre
On a bitin' Jan'ry morn

We passed the weary hebber-man
Until we'd reached the Main
Into heaving waters La Serena sailed
And she were ne'er seen agin

"Luff and touch her!" cried the captain
Did by the westward drift we blow
Towards black alligator waters
Where the mangrove fingers grow

They ripped the sails 'n broke the mast
They tore upon the hull
They drew us down into the swampy
Where we be waitin' still

When the water's still, the moon's a'full
Shining coldy through the moss
We raise the ghost of La Serena
And sing of those that we've lost

I sailed upon the Seven Seas
Long afore ye were ever born
I left you sleepin' in pretty Mary's arms
On a bitin' Jan'ry morn

Beyond The Farallones

With jelly eyes and candied ties
Their coats are sugar spun
Drowning down, the fathoms sound
Until your strugglin's done

They come from
Far beyond the Farallones
In their hovels by the sea
Where no one's home
but Jewel-eyed Joan
Chummy Jack and me

Double, double boil and trouble
How does your garden grow?
On slippery slopes with isotopes
And Devil's Teeth in a row

They come from
Far beyond the Farallones
In their hovels by the sea
Where no one's home
but Jewel-eyed Joan
Chummy Jack and me

A loop-de-loop in the shark fin soup
They'll toss you in the waves
Two by two, in the ole fish coop
Down dig the eggers' graves

They come from
Far beyond the Farallones
In their hovels by the sea
Where no one's home
but Jewel-eyed Joan
Chummy Jack and me

Tsunami

When she rose from the sea
she was not so tall at first:
a playground fountain
the spout of a young whale,
then a skyward climbing
saltwater wall

Sonambulistic Titaness,
roused by the sudden jerk of
the dreaming Vulcan
who shared her seabed

Stirred but not yet awake
in her giantess' slumber,
she rose, gathering the fishing boats –
thorns on her foamy tresses –
the kelp beds, the nurse sharks,
the sea bathers and shipwrecks –
bejeweling her turquoise robes

At her full height, she moved quietly –
saline Colossus, barefooted
advancing over the wrinkled sands
towards the cowering land

And, at the moment, the
sleepwalker opened her eyes,
she tossed her great, blue cape
behind her like a matadora
and retreated, dragging pieces
of the mountains, the reactors,

the harbors, the cities and trees
from the whitewashed day

the helpless thousands,
she carried home like small
souvenirs of a strange dream:
tiny shells, a handful of sand
lost in the pockets of an old coat

Vanishing into the vast gyre,
a gaping mouth to swallow the ocean,
now an oddly spinning anomaly,
now a small, thoughtless splash
where a fisherman tossed a bone

Miranda

The sun rises, burbling
from the lower world
lazily, an egg yolk drips
on the horizon – sultry
summer haze melts in
the orange sherbet sea

Seapink and pickleweed
droop in ripples of heat
rising off the dunes –
beyond the bleached
ribcage of a whale,
the never-surfeited sea is
a seine netful of glinting jewels

My father and I were
set adrift by a jealous uncle;
and by the little lifeboat –
now a carcass rotting–
we found such paradise
where man doth not inhabit

The Moon Was A Ghastly Galleon

The Moon was a ghastly galleon
Tossed on a quicksilver sea
The stars shivered in their wishing wells
On the shoals of Hebrides

The captain was a Black South-Easter
Who blew a blore through the nails
Made splinters of mast and of rudder
And shredded the gossamer sails

The Moon was a ghastly galleon
Tossed on a quicksilver sea
Her crew as all been forsaken
By a whispering Westerly breeze

Tides

The gray morning light,
dull and diffuse,
illuminates purple tie-dyed curtains

her single window
looks out onto rows of
identical houses
so many houses
in all directions
like shingled soldiers
waiting for orders or
for something to change
some news

I think: I have no one to blame
but myself
for bringing her up
in the brutal sameness
of this town, the park
among sickly trees
and brutal boys

no one else to blame
for hoping this life
was a good enough idea
to disturb her
from her peaceful slumber
in a womblike sea

She has been between
the bed and the wall
since dawn;
it is already noon
still gray and formless –

after some pleading, we go to a bookstore
and go home

"Fantastic Voyage"
is on television.
I braid her tangled hair –
Medusa's serpentine locks.
Unexpectedly the news breaks in:

Two Thousand Bodies Wash Ashore With the Tide!
    Japan Now Thirteen Feet Closer!
        Housecat Clings to Clump of Weeds Growing from
                Crack in Concrete Wall!

A Wall of Water is moving
at six hundred miles per hour
towards our own shores

She squeezes my hand;
her head, drooping like a dandelion,
falls upon my shoulder
– my melancholy mermaid

It's so hard to tell what the tide will bring

Hollow Men, Shallow Men

We saw the hollow men
bloom below the eaves
of one hundred spreading branches
from a million fallen leaves

O! Fading Scarlet Waxy Cap
Sweet sylvan lollipop –
You have grown so orange
since last the moon was up

We saw the shallow men
in the sedges near the lake;
they stood with wavering edges
but no shadows did they make

Hey Ho! Great Blue Heron
stealth hunter of the creek –
See the light dance on the ripples,
the silver fish between your feet

III

My Uncles Are Men Of Stones

My uncles, they are men of stones
They bore though root and earth and bones –

Curators of meteorites, purveyors of stalagmites
The sifters of hands in alluvial fans
Quarrymen of granite, prospectors of planets
Sellers of anthracite, champions of the trilobite
Cartographers of aquifers,
Compressors of sand, strippers of land
Black basalt breakers and asphalt bakers
Drillers of cinder cones, explorers of diatoms
Drivers of dunes on Jovian moons

Uncles, tell me —
How sets God by sand the shifts of time?
By stone, his mortal clock?

> *Alas, dear niece, though we be men*
> *It's best to ask the rocks.*

My aunts, they are women of mysteries
And blood-clotted histories –

Diviners of waters, makers of daughters
Tealeaf readers, witch-burned healers
Spreaders of seeds, collectors of reeds
Pickers of berries, communing with faeries
Bad omen tellers, pale sub-lake dwellers
Mountain top prophets, stuffers of pockets
Brewers of stews made from frog-spleen and newts
Dead rune rewriters, Amazonian fighters
Ionian dwellers and fiddlehead sellers

Aunts, tell me —
How speaks God in dreams of ancient things?
His mind in leaves of tea?

> *Alas, dear niece, we listen naught*
> *But to the rocking of the sea.*

Radiant City

When the woman fell through
the crack in the city sidewalk
she fell many fathoms
towards a radiant abyss
there were so many women
down in the crystal caves
they had been falling through
the cracks for so long

The women made a city near
the vents where the blue light
of bioluminescent animals
lit up the long nights
they walked quietly in the sparkling
salt pillar forests, gathering
in the flowing flora, collecting
honey from the honeyfish's mouth

After they had been there a while
a few wished to swim in the subterranean
sea; and so they grew gills and tales
with prismic, adamantine scales

Soon women fell like rain through
the cracks in the city sidewalks
which are said to cover over
nearly two percent of the Earth
but nobody missed them

Whenever a man went missing
through the cracks, the other
men would search the manholes

They did not see the radiant city
nor do they hear the mermaids
singing softly to the fallen, turning them
gently into pillars of salt with their lullabies

The Living Bridges Of Megahlaya

Wiser than the hills, the old woman lives
above the monsoon waters, beyond the high
cliff wall where the living bridges stretch and die
over centuries in the Valley of Megahlaya;

With her high knuckled hands and sinewy,
nimble fingers she bends the groping roots
of the Strangler Fig, tying them to others
when the river runs low and the wood is supple

Her daughter and her granddaughter
perform this work, day in and day out

They require no machines or engineers
Just the weaver's art and a keen sense of eternity

The Orphan

That night in Paris, I slept in the belfry;
It was a church much smaller than Notre Dame
Where Hugo's laboring hunchback, full of shame,
Brought his Gypsy Queen in under the law of sanctuary

That night in Paris, as I lay hidden under Heaven's gaze;
French moths fluttered about in the open windows
Where, with the first falling of winter snows,
I watched the pirouettes of paper dancers on a moonlit stage

That night in Paris, I thought of the "little sparrow"
Singing for her supper in the filthy streets, penniless,
And how she, for a while was blind
but in a whore's warm embrace
Felt motherly love to be an unguided arrow

That night in Paris, I looked down upon a small streetside café
Where two young lovers drank red wine,
Staring, like hands of clock towards three and nine,
Indifferently towards the belfry, where I lie alone awake

That night in Paris, because of my poverty,
Sister Ann held my hand, and told me the story
Of her love for the great Archangel Gabriel;
Since I had no name and could not read or spell,

And because she had been so kind to me
In honor of both him and of her
In honor of Paris, my own beloved City,
I took, for myself, a name – L'Anarchie

IV

The Blue-Skinned Man

'Ban, 'Ban, Ca-Caliban!
The blue-skinned man
is a Fungus Fan;
He's the Holy See
of mycology,
He's the Mushroom Man
from a far-away land

When I went a strolling
Below the forest rainbow,
The blue-skinned man told me:
"Careful where your feet go –

'Ban, 'Ban, Ca-Caliban!
The blue-skinned man
is a Fungus Fan;
He's the Holy See
of mycology,
He's the Mushroom Man
from a far-away land

"I'm a fungus in the dead logs,
A mushroom in the roots;
I'm a truffle in the ground
So be wary of your boots!"

Skip a rope, jump a rope,
        get in line–
How many mushrooms
        can you find?

Ravenel's Stinkhorn
    Deadly Galerina
Turkey Tail, Inky Cap
    Bleeding Mycena
Dead Man's Fingers
    Strangulated Amanita

Dryad's Saddle
    Dung-loving Psilocybe
Beefsteak Polypore
    Poison Pie
Witch's Butter
    Club-footed Clitocybe

Orange Milky, Panther
    Shaggy Parasol
Witch's Hat, Death Cap
    False Chanterelle

Destroying Angel
    The King and Slippery Jack
Swamp Beacon, Dry Rot
    Fading Scarlet Waxy Cap

Fawn and Pleated Puffballs
    Ochre Spreading Tooth
Old Man of the Woods
    Pig's Ear and Velvet Foot

Devil's Urn and Sulphur Shelf
    Sweating, Sweetbreads
If the blue-skinned man
    catches you, you're DEAD!

        (jumper goes out)

In Another Life

In another's other life
In another other's land
Tree roots grew in cellars
When our mouths were full of sand.

The sky rained maple syrup
When the gargoyle choir sang –
The clouds were made of gypsum
As the rusted church bells rang.

The Minotaur taught Sunday school
The Griffin skipped a rope –
The serpent in the steeple
Drank tea of lyme and soap.

In another other life
In other nother lands
The grass was grown from silent seeds,
When our mouths were full of sand.

Jump Rope Rhyme Of The Moirae

Clotho was a girl
from the land beyond the dead;
From her distaff to her spindle
she spun a deadly thread;
Pull it once, pull it twice
> Then toss the bony dice –
If she cuts it in the middle
> Your baby's cold as ice!
Jump rope girls, they speak in rhymes
Jump rope girls, they must keep time

Lachesis, she says,
"I draw the lots!"
With her wicked measure-stick
she'll put you in the plot.
Measure once, measure twice
> Toss the bony dice –
If you draw a short stick
> Your mama's cold as ice!
Jump rope girls, they speak in rhymes
Jump rope girls, they must keep time

Atropos stole the scissors from
her gramma's sewing basket;
If she cuts your string in half
you'll end up in a casket.
Snip it once, snip it twice
> Toss the bony dice –
Say your last good-bye *(jumper goes out)*
> Cuz your daddy's cold as ice!
Jump rope girls, they speak in rhymes
Jump rope girls, they keep your time

Once I Was Queen of a Rubbish Heap

I found the words *sunless rivers weep*
Their waves into the deep
Etched on wave-worn seagreen glass,
Lost in blades of dry brown grass
Where she'd slept a secret *charmed sleep*

Now I am here in her *rosy morn;*
Among her fields of planted corn
I hear footsteps of her phantom feet
Along forgotten lanes of mossy peat
That led the way through barb and thorn

Tho Sadness was her sweet *nightingale*
Joy was passing through her veil
And Quietness was her *purple land*
Where she'd written with her snow-white hand
To all the Goblin Market men: We here are not for sale.

The Wide Sufficing Sea

The sufficing sea reflects
       – wavering, awake and vague –
On darker, earlier, wilder wrecks

The sea, an abstraction made of air
       – wavering and vaguely awake –
Condemns the insistence of electric chairs

The bombs rush

Entering profound, condemning depths
       – parts of broken bottles –
Insisting towards earlier, darker wrecks

Descend like treeless pinnacles, which
       – having made themselves scarce –
Approach death, through the wavering water

Weather Vane

While the weight is equal on each
side of the weather vane,
the surface area is divided in unequal parts
allowing the pointer to move
freely on its axis
in wind

Weather vanes are generally decorative,
often featuring the traditional cockeral
with letters indicating the points
of the instrument known as
the compass

The side with the larger surface area is blown away
from the wind direction so that the smaller side
with the pointer, is pivoted to face
the direction of the wind,
and so spins accordingly

Most weather vanes have markers beneath
the arrow, aligned with the lines on the earth.

Weather vanes with fanciful shapes, do not always
betray the direction of a very gentle wind –
often figures do not achieve the exact design balance
and yet, it is sometimes wise to remember,

Whimsy has no need of direction

V

Monstrous Teachers

Recently, while spell checking the name of bad beer
      – an American pisswater pastime
I discovered Schlitzie the Pinhead,
because that's how a search engines work;
they surprise you with monstrous teachers

Then I couldn't help but read on;
Schlitizie, otherwise known as Simon Metz
had made some instant impression on me
a long time ago

His face was familiar, Jewish parents
most likely, poor, lived in the Bronx –
we might have been related, immigrant freaks;

His heart was as big as his head was small
as I read I recalled how Schlitzie couldn't speak;
he wore dresses called "frocks,"
and was suspected of being female
as if that were a crime

only those close to him knew
dresses made it easier to keep him
clean and comfortable when he wet himself

Schlitzie, that you remained forever,
a four-year old, and were probably
sold to the circus by someone who had

clearly taken loving, adoring care of you but
could no longer afford to keep you made my
heart seize. Did you despair as I do now?

how is it these same monsters I go hunting for
for under boulders of memory – harpies, hags,
hunchbacks, witches, prophetic wretches

these monsters that inhabit the dark woods
of my dreams, plague my stories – they
show me myself, then recoil from me

I pull them screaming from their blissful graves
suture them to my cruel words, give them
unfamiliar homes, new agonies – yet

they were some mother's beloved child;
they were some father's bottomless shame;
they were brothers, sisters – bothersome and blessed

Schlitzie, when they sent you to a facility
and you were discovered by the sword swallower
who was working as an off-season ward –

lost member of an alien race, bedwetting "Aztec,"
microcephalic freak, dress-wearing monkey

Schlitize, did your old-friend-the-sword-swallower
grieve so at your innocent despair that he brought
you home? Did you remain a child until –

Schlitze, you died in 1971
at which time hundreds of thousands
of American soldiers, millions of Vietna –

in that year I was four; we had our first
black and white television; officers
came and went from our house, all stoned

Schlitzie, I must have seen you on television
when all those Vietnamese children were dying,
to remember your dumb smile so well now

Still Life With Object(s)

Like the famous ship
at the edge of the continent –
the one the Indians never saw
although it was right in front of them –
I wonder how long I have lived
among these people who were,
until now, this moment,
broken headphones, steel wool
a flash mob, a throbbing headache

We know them.
Lampooning behind mirrored masks
of debris in a car wash puddle –
Jiffy Lube coupons, a jay's wing
a bent Big Gulp straw
a twist tie, an oil sheen
discarded bottles,
pills and perfumed soaps
pass unaltered from us
into the coursing waterways
making amphibians female
as they go, killing freshwater mussels
those keepers of the rivers'
clear waters all these eons and we
didn't know until now
how things forever alter.

I cannot re-enchant the world
myself, inert and alone;
in my house
the dishwasher hums

the toilet sings
the radiator knocks; outside
the chainsaw, the leafblower,
the shop vac, the lawnmowers
drown the sounds
the shrill laughter
of children swinging

A small honey mushroom is growing
between my toes, it is
beginning to discompose my
feet on the spot where I stand
suddenly awake
listening to all these people here;
soon the microbes of the forest floor
will migrate through the rotten
webbing, through my limbs
on which the crows alight.

I, like a tree.
Now the things in my house,
gathering, flammable armies beneath
garbage mountains, flotillas of objects
the size of Texas, the greenhouse breath
they assemble, are on the move
singing, humming, knocking, flowing
while I listen to the rasping of
a diasporic wind

The Quotidian Inferno

Waiting at the fiery gates
of The Quotidian Inferno,
our guide, a young Greek in vintage Pumas,
says he goes by P. V. Maro.
He's got something to show us.

"Nine levels of scary, a dark wood and
a Satanic freak show at the end.
Don't worry about the pets, they don't bite.
I know the way through the joint,
up to a point. Or down to one."

It's bigger than the Mall of America,
And darker than the Chunnel Tunnel.
Even if it smells of sorrow and rotten luck,
your curiosity overtakes you.
"For a few bucks," says our guide,
"Get a personal, behind-the-scenes tour
of the garden of earthly delights!"

A carnal carnival, a dark themed park –
centaurs stand knee-deep
in the shallow rapids of bloody rivers
among the bobbing heads of killers
to ensure their suffering is eternal.
"It scares the stuff out of the living,"
says P.V. Maro with the vintage Pumas.

"At the Apothecary, one finds
remedies for dropsy, drops for Gluttony
cooling agents for Lust, elixirs for Avarice,

leeches for Violence, placebos for Fraud
snake oil for Greed and a stinging nettle
mouthwash, special-made for Heresy.
In the Quotidian Inferno Funhouse
you can walk across burning sands
and talk to the Harpies about
your marital problems; your
Congressman is shaking hands
at the Lake of Boiling Pitch, where his
molasses fingers trade in dark sticky secrets."

Sensing the sale was going nowhere,
P.V. Maro had a change of heart:
"There's another joint across the strip –
if you want, half-way between here and
the Contrapasso, just past the Acheron,
'The Garden Variety Paradise!'
Nice place, good food, clean fun."

"Funny," he says, lighting a cigarette,
"but it never draws a crowd."

The Young Master and the Lotus

The girl presents the painting she holds
in her small, stained hands; she
blows hard upon the still-wet canvass –
peachy, freckled, puffer fish cheeks

A yellow tulip with red-outlined petals
two-toned, green leaves open
from the short stem like welcoming
hands in small mittens

A single bloom in the foreground
Growing on a round, brown hillock
Striated with red streaks – some genus
That grows sideways

Dark, billowing storm clouds gather
In the background
Seabirds whirl in a Phthalo blue sky –
A lonely place to plant bulbs

"What a bright tulip!" I say
"It must be springtime on this island."
"This is not a tulip," she frowns.
"It is the lotus of the Goddess Kuan Yin!"

"Oh, of course, the Lotus of Kuan Yin! –
Many apologies," I bow.
"Her lotus grows on the Island," she says
"of Red Thorns; it is far, far away.

Kuan Yin is the Goddess of Compassion,
which this young master will need
because I have just seen red, sideways fingerprints
On the white, hallway walls

Star Thistle

At the End
only Star Thistle grew
along the roads we knew

Barbed seeds pierced our soles
the sun baked dry crackers
of the summer fields of wheat
in pulsing waves
of liquid heat

At the End
when every oily bead
of ink-black mead
was siphoned from the floor
drained from the vast, slow-shifting sea,
our mouths were hungry holes
bleating in the beating sun
More! More! Ever more!

At the End
when the deadly Jimson Weed
grown from dead dirt seed
killed the cattle
fattend on foreign grass,
watered with gasoline –
the wells were dry and empty yet,
our famine fed by deep regret

At the End
in those final stifling days
through windows glazed
with sulphured haze,
we watched the red skies burn –

Skies of the Evening Star
glowing bright with Beauty's name

In the End
our fate might have been the same
if were not for HOPE –

        joker in the lot
        pink petal in the blackened pot

But of course, all along we knew;
and so our shoes
were boiled and chewed

The Gravedigger

A ground beetle digs
Uprooting plastic bouquets
Under mossy oaks

Speckled Fawns

The fawns, unmoving
Hide in their new spotted coats
In the dappled light

Dream Of Water

The winter stream runs
Past pearly mushrooms on trees
And ferns on boulders

Ascension

Late July evening–
blown about by fans, crane flies knock
Against the ceiling

Outskirts, Summer

Bottle flies abuzz
In the tall, pointed shadows
Of orange traffic cones

Speeding Bullets

From asphalt vapors
Burning apparitions speed–
Silver tanker trucks

De Poésie Ou De Vertu

We have a beautiful plaza in this town,
Laid out by a Mexican commandante when the land
Belonged to one man or another, all according to plan –
But the hundred-year-old trees were planted by women

Here, in the valley of the moons,
Stale references are made to Jack London and Bacchus
But few to the raving ones, the Maenads – perhaps because
Everyone here drinks wine, yet so few read poetry?

I make it a habit of always bringing a book
Of poetry, or a French novel to read
On autumn afternoons when the yellow Gingko leaves
Fall like golden rain upon the children swinging

Just last week I saw a girl, twenty if she was a day
Reading my favorite book of Baudelaire's prose poems –
The one called *Twenty Prose Poems by Baudelaire*–
Under the quiet shade of the great Southern Magnolia

And what caught my attention first was the cover,
As hers was a library book, which ruled out
Some possibilities: for example, the book wasn't a gift
From an East Coast cousin studying in Paris

It isn't a book one finds at a yard sale or flea market
Nor something she would've discovered snooping
In her mother's lock box of forgotten treasures –
Old love letters, odd trinkets saved from a former life

It wasn't a book the local bookstore owner on the square
Would have recommended; he'd freely admit
His taste is more Chabon or Roth; he has little interest
In nonsense about the moon's curse on a green-eyed girl

I wanted to ask the girl if she knew why the French adore Poe, or
What she thought of "Double Chamber" or "Favours of the Moon"
And if she'd read *In Search of Lost Time*; but I stopped,
Sheepishly fearing she might guess I read translations

From across the sandbox, I saw that she had long brown hair
And was narrow through the hips, like I once was,
And was dressed in old jeans, worn sneakers and a sweatshirt
Just fashionable enough not to be noticed at all

When she rose to leave, she pulled the hood over her face;
To avoid lingering in a strange man's imagination, fearing
He should keep some part of her, she passed phantom-like
Through rippling autumn light, through falling golden leaves

As she was leaving there were things I wanted to say:
Stay away from tone-deaf Troubadors
who strum for your attention out of tune
Even when you're trying to read French poetry in bed, and
Don't wear shoes you can't run fast in – you just never know

There were so many things I wanted to tell the girl
Who walked quietly away under the yellow paper rain,
But all I knew to say in French was: "enivrez-vous sans cesse!
De vin, de poésie ou de vertu, à votre guise."

NOTE: "enivrez-vous sans cesse!/De vin, de poésie ou de vertu, à votre guise" are lines from Baudelaire's prose poem "Enivrez-Vous" or "Get Drunk." (City Lights Books)

Kehoe

Once I was Afraid.
There was that greasy stain
On the gold-quilted bedspread, and
At the front desk, the aging redhead
Who chain-smoked and spoke
Through a hole in her throat,
With that hand-held machine –
How her voice seemed
Like a phantom in the electrical line,
Cold-calling from the other side
Of the rumbling overpass
Where shards of broken glass
Lay like teeth in sharp brown grass –
Do remember how we screamed?
When the tan van with dark windows
And the eight-track tape deck playing
Dream Weaver like it was underwater?
The roach burning in the ashtray,
And how he stayed and waited
Until the rancid haze of daylight
Begot that stifling night
Moth-frenzied under the streetlight
Flickering and buzzing, insects teaming,
There were bee bees in the shag carpet
In that van – bee bees of all things.
Do you remember that place on I-5?
There, when I was still alive,
By the Interstate?

* * *

Now I am Here.
Joy is a cottage by the beach
Made from stone and whitewashed
With a roof, thatched and sun-bleached;
Nearby the nuthatch and scrub jay
Steal planted seeds and snap peas
From the rich loam under stepping-stones;
The wailing of the Least Terns
Over distant breakers that pound and churn;
The Quail, so loyal and so humble
Scurry in and out through bramble.
Those fragrant vines of sweet, pink jasmine,
Bold bougainvillea and clematis
Climb the old iron rungs.
In the driftwood chimes, the cool Pacific
Sings light, unhurried songs
A hearth fire of fallen logs burns
Dried kindling from the underbrush;
The gentle Hermit Thrush
Is always out my window.
In the morning I will go –

Through stands of thistle and sea-fig
And footsteps-of spring
The sea-thrift and the cream cups
A cacophony of birdsong rises up
With the scent of crushed mint in the mid-day heat,
In dissonant but perfect melody.

This place where things, like dreams, can be unmade –
Now I am here, and not afraid.

Jerusalem Cricket

Once, (when I was drowning in a swimming pool)
a boy scooped me out
with the net and
dumped me on the wet,
concrete deck

just in time for the housecat
to spot me crawling
towards the dirt –
so dark and cool

In Mexico, you know,
I am called El Bebe de la Tierra

because of an uncanny
resemblance I have
to a fetus

I have quite a nasty bite
for a wingless
cricket
and inflicted two
upon the housecat
just before he batted me
back into the pool

The Locusts

I climb the stairs.
I have been waiting in mute darkness
In these nests below the desert hardpan.
I hear the moving black waters that bear
The dead towards the wide river mouth –
The Sea of Eternal Return.

There is a door on the desert floor –
I climbed through it once before.
I enter the desert with sun-blinded eyes;
My skin begins to crack, my heart swells.
Soon, very tired, I will step out of this old shell,
Which was so painfully confining, and undersized.

I hope, dimly, that I will find a new story here,
That the pale blue sky will be clear,
With a promise in the summer wind
Of a chance to begin again.

The sky darkens. A rank stench.

I look out over the desert –
Strewn, like billions of waxy doubles,
Are the brittle remains of molted bodies.

The new humans swarm in a black cloud overhead.
Ready to descend again –
These have wings.

House Finches

The tall stalks of anise weed
Sway in the field like fronds
in a shallow pond from which
the water has turned to mist
under the weak winter sun

House finches pry the seeds
from the late dying weeds
come up in autumn

The only traces of the old farm
its rich soil was buried alive
by sidewalks, roads and houses
are the anise weeds that burst forth
from the memory of good earth
in the last open field

Sealed in and suffocated
by small patches of poison lawns;
The owner of the last open field
ran a tractor through in June
and dispersed the very
thing he sought to eradicate –
And now, in winter.
the house finch comes to celebrate

So many houses – houses all the same
their windows blink indifferently
In the weak, dying sun of winter

So many little finches
flitter about – seedhead to seedhead
and take to sudden scattered flight.
flushed by the arrival of the
neighbor's pitiless housecat

VI

A Wine Country Murder Mystery
In Three Parts

I - The Dutch Finger Prince

They came in on a harvest moon,
A King and Queen from Holland
And their only son, a simpleton,
Heard singing in the vineyards

He went to taste the wine alone
But a peasant girl, watching vultures
Near the fallen oak, waiting, swaying
Wings splayed in a Reaper's cloak,

Said the bird's head was a scrotum;
Indeed, he said the head of the bird
Was red and wrinkled and thinly feathered
They laughed together and drank the wine

The stonemason, a simple man,
Heard singing in the vineyards
As the son went down, the moon rose and night fell
He left his handiwork on a high note

But his fingers shone red, red, red
Underneath the harvest moon
When metal dripped the drops on stones
As the notes fell and the crickets chirped

She, barefooted
Had wanted to go home
From pruning, picking, kissing, singing,
From cutting vines and drinking wine

The crime scene was different than the crime seen…

The stonemason had "heard only chirping"
In the vineyards
When the grapes were picked
And vines were cut

No matter, Cloggy Boy, said the peasant cop
To the prince — Veins are not dykes!
Fingers cannot stop wine that overflows
From those who sing and prune

Prints of fingers on cold, cut stones
That ran along the bone, dry creek…
But the Queen and King and son had come
Only for the harvest wine

Before the red stains mixed with greasy spots
In the gravel of a parking lot,
For the King and Queen
Who'd come just to taste the wine

Told the stone mason for a pound of gold
Vultures bled on stones
And dust might bury bones
Of those hurt singing in the vineyards

II – The Stonemason's Wife

As she poured the oil into the lamps
The stonemason's wife was waiting
The soup was stirred and thin
The bones were boiled clean

He'd gone to lay the stones at dawn
The sun was hot
The grapes were picked
The peasant girl was singing, pruning

Her feet were bare, the stones were hot
The only son had gone alone
He'd never tasted ripened fruit
He'd never been in love before

Sometimes she stepped upon his spine
So cracked and broken from laying stone
She sang and made the bones lay straight
Under eyes and wings of birds that waited

The mason's wife was cold and waiting
The soup was thin and bones were bare
A pound of gold for a side of bacon
A wheel of cheese, the harvest wine

The crime seen was not a criminal offense…

The dancing drinking led to lying
The pruning knife in the apron pocket
The veins were cut, the wine was spilled
The drops on stones were evidence

The pound of gold for a broken back
The hand-laid cottage made of stone
The soup was cold.
The wife went in to pick the bones

The crickets chirped
The wife was picking, cleaning, stirring
Serving soup too thin, thin, thin
The harvest moon was waiting, watching

Should Kings and Queens and simple sons
Drink harvest wines in golden cups
When peasant girls, with bare, wine feet
Ceased their singing, stomping in the vineyards?

The mason's wife set down the soup
He, the bag of gold
They drank the red, red, peasant wine
And praised God for singing in the vineyards

And red stains mixed with greasy spots
In the gravel of parking lots,
And Kings and Queens
Who come just to taste the wine

III – The Widow's Harvest

The stonemason's wife was shelling beans
The peasant cop stopped by to chat
How had she money for the harvest wines
The wheel of cheese, the bacon fat?

His shoes were dusty, the sun was hot
The grapes were picked, the harvest done
The peasant girl who pruned and cut
Had left some rows of vines to rot

The King and Queen had a simple son
He told the wife, who scattered seeds
They'd come to taste the harvest wines
The son had never been alone

The pruning knife in the dry creek bed
The hand that touched the bloody drops
Had left a mark upon the stones
When the notes fell and the crickets chirped

The son, the peasant cop was kicking dust,
In his youthful innocence,
From a fire picked up burning stones
His fingertips were smooth as bone

When he heard singing in the vineyards
He'd gone to taste the wine alone
He'd never been in love before
But a prince's prints weren't left on stones

The crime scene betrayed the crime seen…

The peasant cop left her pulling weeds;
A stack of wood left by the walls of stone
Was home to a widow, round and black
The mason's back was nearly broke

He lay upon a bed of straw
In a cup of stone, the widows' fate
The stonemason's soup was fat and hot
The harvest wine was sweet and red

A cup of stone, beneath his head
A kiss upon the vein
When the vines were pruned and the grapes were picked
And peasant girls, who sang and kissed were cut

Under dust and blood of birds
The stonemason saw a burning sun
The wine did not flow
The vines did not grow

But the mason's widow took down the stones
Made her home from the fallen oak
Under wings and watching moons
Like eyes of barefoot peasant girls
Hurt singing, singing in the vineyards

VII

The Nightjar (Alba)

A whippoorwill sings
Her bright, nocturnal song
Into the fading light of evening.
Near her nest, hidden among the rushes,
Lie lovers, warm and unhindered
In rustic dens of dull colored leaves,
Where the crimson palpitations
Of beating hearts and kiss-closed eyes
Are soon startled by a cock's crow,
And the discovering sunrise
That catches, if only for a moment,
The departing of souls.

Our Last Speakeasy Days

Old Hoagy Carmichael, said times were but the dregs
That old 'bang of bad booze, flappers with bare legs
Jingle jangle morals and them wild weekends'
And the bird bones rattled in an ancient dance

Gone the swinging doors, and the old spittoons
gone the red, dim rooms of MacCready's Olde Saloon
Where Death dealt diamonds to Fate and Chance
And the bird bones rattled in an ancient dance

Gone the dance hall girls, the Jack pine boardwalk
Gone the player piano and the Firewater shots
In come the bootleggers, a Tanglefoot romance
And the bird bones rattle in an ancient dance

In come devil's candy, bathtub gin and hooch
In come Bozeman Betty – wooden nickels for a smooch
In come the Devil with a password and a prance
And still the bird bones rattled in an ancient dance

A Brief History Of Mirrors

As a small child she remembered
pulling the mirror down with the linen
cloth on her grandmother's vanity, and
how it shattered on the floor; she
recalled staring at the scattered shards,
the surprised look of a hundred
identical faces trapped in a plane,
gazing back in wonder; she wondered
who was the real Asteria

She learned certain things about
the history of mirrors, such as:
when light falls on a body, some
quantity of light is reflected, some
is absorbed, and some is transmitted
through the body; a mirror works
by virtue of smoothness lest the
light be scattered and diffused,
and lost to the blackness of space

She learned certain things about
the history of stars, such as:
the light from the Sun, the
closest star, reaches earth in eight
and three tenths minutes; yet, other
stars are so far away they have
already died by the time their distant
light reaches the small mirrors
inside the telescopes on Earth

When she was older, Asteria broke
a mirror and glued the small pieces
to her body; she walked about
under the bright Sun for many days
in the hopes that the fading light of her life
might travel across the cosmos
with the small chance of being seen by a
young girl on a distant planet who might
mistake Asteria for a very small star

A Brief History Of Echoes

Womanhood had come to her in a
warzone, after the time when
the dune grasses and the dry chaparral
had been cleared and scorched,
the wetlands drained and the creeks diverted
around the undulated greens,
all making way for the terracotta villas –
those uncanny colonies crawling as far
as the naked eye could see and beyond

she left the sea for a high hilltop cave
she sang into the void, listening
for the song of hydrogen

For many years, she heard only voices of
Machines, the blood-curdling anthems of tyrants,
the shrieking of their terracotta villa wives
who, after French manicures, Thai massages
after juice of dandelions and burdock roots,
after holding a benefit to benefit
the last polar bears and running caribou, now
needing new homes in the lower states
because pipelines need straight lines –
she heard the sound of Nothing for the first time

Nearby on far-off Io, interstellar sirens
heard her gentle song echoing in their
Jovian conk shells, and they were moved

they pulled the anchor of their iron rock
set a course for the small spinning sapphire
of a small Anthemoessan sphere

breaking the sound waves with their
cold frequencies Circe, fierce captain,
traaced a lonely current and piloted
the great rock across oceans of eternal night

sailing fearlessly, the ship broke the ice fields
of Saturn's rings with its mighty iron hulls
past an army of wax-eared sentinels and into
the eye of earth's perfect storm of unlistening

Over time, the iron oxide dust on her plastic
skin began to rearrange itself, and so
the ambient terracotta villa Muzak piped in
through holes in the houses of the Lotus Eaters
became both Requiem and Prelude
inaudible to all except her, there,
listening from her hilltop cave to the silent void
with nothing but a small human heart

She, shopworn oracle, foresaw the next age –
it began with a wind chime in the driftwood rafters
with the shape of laughter in the darkness
with the hushabye of pine needles on a granite peak,
with the ring of a monk's singing bowl washed up with
the debris of the evening's plastic tide

It would begin with the whistling wind in
the wasted pipe miles of organs laid in oily tundra
where the metal had rotted, and the curious wind,
blowing around the bones of the polar bears
and the caribou and of the cannibal men
whispered of changes not yet known

Humming softly to this ancient song
suddenly recalled in stillness
the woman made a small fire for
Our Ladies of the Iron Rock
who were so weary from their journey

VIII

Laconia

When you are in the Underworld, you may travel for many days over barren, windswept plains before you come to a lake; this is the Lake of Memories. Untie the small boat on the sandy bank and row out. Do not fear the vapors – you have already been here.

Some may look into the deep green waters of the Lake and see below its quicksilvered surface a luminescent city where white marble towers rise up from sparkling, pyrite sands. You may see the remnants of old fields and forests, ruined ramparts, and stone fortresses. This may be your homeland: the Citadel of Long-Forgotten Dreams. Or it may all be real and the people are all drowned.

You may, however, catch a glimpse of another sort of place, quite different and yet vaguely, eerily familiar. This is the House of Shadows. For years you have tried hard to forget the black, liquid dreams of this place. It was not the only house of childhood but the one where the darkness seeped in.

The Lake may take up your cause and cloud the water with sediment or trouble the surface with a sudden squall, but still, you will strain to see. You cannot quite bring the house into focus in the churning murkiness. In your frustration and insatiable desire to wander the submerged corridors, you may jump in. Never say we didn't warn you.

By some magic, you will breathe underwater. You descend through the green depths and swim slowly through the threshold of the front door, patched together with a pine board and tacks and scratch-marked by the dog as it had been then.

You will swim through the dark hallway, the empty dining room, peek into that small back bathroom you are still afraid of ever since someone climbed through the tiny window when you weren't home and stole your mother's wallet. You will gaze through the living room windows, fogged from the cool night air – those windows with the thin metal frames and broken cranks that neither open nor close windows.

Like a ghost that peers into the realm of the living but sees only the dying, you will stare out the living room window, the one your mother never covered with curtains or shades even though it looked out into an unpenetrable riparian wall of poplars and bays and the densely wooded hillside beyond.

When you recall how you felt always watched and how naked the three of you were, alone in a thriftshop fishbowl, abandoned in the empty world, you will forget you are drowning. You will see the dog scratching her fleas on a front lawn of green seagrass. She will bark ferociously at the black, leafless trees in the watery woods because you could not.

When you are in the Underworld, you will remember how the dog whined when your father made a rare appearance. You will see the torn mattress on the floor where you slept and catch a glimpse of the wavering silhouette of your father stumbling through the doors, his breath sour with whiskey, sliding silver dollars under your pillow when you pretended you were asleep, and you will know it is Christmas.

You will swim through and through the rooms of the house over the rotting brown shag carpet, past the broken locks and windows and you will get a true picture of your poverty.

When you look under the house at your old hiding place in the crawl space among the mildewed Samsonites and black widows, the dog will appear to you again. Her whimpering will remind you of how many times you hid there on the cold ground and how she never gave you away and also how hard that betrayal was for her because your father loved the dog too. And you will see now that she was only a dog, after all.

You may swim towards the surface to get a better view of the neighborhood, to get a little perspective. The light is better there and so you will see certain things with refreshing clarity: the neighbors, swaying like tules, still poised as if ready at any minute to resume their scandalous gossiping about your family in that wooded canyon where to be poor and broken was to shatter their shared delusion.

You will float through the front door, down the potholed afterthought of a road known as Evergreen "Not A County Maintained Road," Lane, past the house where the boy named Byron who'd earned a reputation for eating raw bacon once shot his bee bee gun from his bedroom window at your mother as she was walking wearily home from work in the twilight, carrying the groceries because her car had been repossessed. Like your lives.

When you are in the Underworld, your vision will be bleary, the images wavering. Yet, when you see the white stucco wall of the house behind your own, built on a higher ground (such a hideous house!) to capture the light of the sun, which penetrated like a prison yard searchlight into your dark kitchen, you may want to leave, to swim away.

Like someone pointing the reflected sunlight from a mirror into your soul – long-hibernating in the secret darkness – you will see now how the cruel light illuminates nothing. Really, you will wonder, who builds chalk white houses in the deep woods? You will recall instead how that prison yard searchlight pulled you out of your hiding places by the hair and made you tremble under its cold imperial gaze, its unhumanity. It is the White Wall of Annihilation. In the cool green waters of the lake, the reflection off the high, blank, windowless wall of the uphill neighbor's cruel white house will not shimmer and waver like the brick house where you lived. It will blind you with its ugly, indifference.

Yet if you look away from the wall, you will see traces of the evening sun sparkling through the translucent, green-yellow leaves floating down from the towering poplars that grow along the creek. You will remember how the breeze made that gentle hushing sound through the leaves and pine needles and whispered secrets you could not understand.

You will drift on a gentle current towards the creek where those poplars grow. You will see the place where you hid in the undergrowth or stomped in too-big borrowed waders during winter rains. You may look back and see the faint outline of your mother, with her long black hair, high cheekbones and gray-green eyes, smoking cigarettes under the rotting, falling shingles of the carport.

You may hear the faint sound of crying. It is your mother, lamenting her wasted youth, her wasted life. You will swim frantically upstream towards her with an urgent message – how sorry you are to have been such a burden! But she is already gone. The water held her gaze too long, and she has vanished into the depths.

You will float wearily towards the old house again – the house of your girlhood, the Shipwreck of Your Soul – and rest for a while on the last solid branch of the old cherry tree, the Tree of Forgiveness. You will remember how sweet the cherries were, and how you once tried to save a bird that had flown into a window the year the windows were washed.

The same bird is watching from the roof. It descends and hops about merrily at the end of the branch where you sit comfortably near the trunk, the place where the branch is strongest. Eventually you will earn the little bird's trust and it will eat the ripe, deep red cherries from your hand.

You will remember then that the bird had died and you will no longer believe any of what you have seen; your memories lap upon the Shores of Time and expire. You will hear, faintly, your mother laughing at your sister, who always could make your mother laugh with her funny little, bird dance.

In time, after you have eaten the sweet, deep-red cherries and watched the gentle fluttering of the poplar leaves that catch the last rays golden sunlight, shimmering in that fleeting moment, you will swim silently away with one last breath in your lungs towards the River of Forgetfulness.

www.ingramcontent.com/pod-product-compliance
Lightning Source LLC
Chambersburg PA
CBHW022020290426
44109CB00015B/1248